Investing

The Comprehensive Educational Program For Novices To Master Proficient Trading Techniques Incorporating The Optimal Strategies To Enhance Revenue Generation

Stewart Dupuis

TABLE OF CONTENT

Dividends And Stock Prices

Within the majority of organizations, fluctuations in stock prices have insignificant influence on the dividend payouts that shareholders receive. In this manner, you can allocate your funds to specific stocks with the confident foresight of the exact amount of annual passive income you will accrue. For example, in the event of a sudden decline in the stock price, the dividend payment for a specific period remains unaffected, ensuring that you still receive it as income. Companies adjust their dividend allocations in accordance with their financial circumstances and the prevailing market conditions. A company experiencing financial difficulties is likely to reduce the dividend payout.

There exists a variety of dividend stocks, and prior to engaging in any purchases, it is imperative to possess thorough comprehension of the market's available options. Dividend stocks can be categorized into three distinct types: stocks with low yields, stocks with medium yields, and stocks with high yields. Low yielding stocks refer to those that produce a rate of return that is below the mean dividend yield. On average, this typically amounts to 2% or less. Investing in such stocks carries substantial risk, as their survival during inflationary periods is exceedingly rare. In the event that the stock demonstrates inadequate performance within the market, it is possible that dividends will not be received from stocks with diminished yield. Stocks with a moderate level of yield are those that exhibit a yield approximately 3% higher than the average yield of the index.

Corporations that possess these stocks distribute dividends constituting 30 to 50 percent of their earnings. When these stocks are exchanged, it is likely that you will receive your dividends. Highly profitable stocks are characterized by a dividend yield of considerable magnitude. These investments offer a reliable source of passive income as the payment of dividends is consistently assured.

Dollar Cost Averaging

Allow us to commence our analysis by examining a method of safeguarding ourselves from systemic risk, although it should be noted that this strategy does not primarily intend to serve that objective. Dollar cost averaging confers various benefits upon us.

The initial approach employed by seasoned investors, which all prospective purchasers of dividend stocks should consider incorporating into their stock-buying practices, is known as dollar cost averaging. The objective of this strategy is to mitigate the inherent volatility of the stock market by balancing out its fluctuations in the long run. This encompasses recessions and booms, which despite their intensity in the moment, will appear comparatively insignificant when viewed in the context of long-term trends retrospectively.

In essence, the stock market is replete with fluctuations in value. What this implies is that prices are experiencing swift and unpredictable fluctuations, oscillating between upward and downward movements. The primary objective of implementing a dollar cost averaging strategy is to mitigate the influence of market volatility on your buying power. Dollar cost averaging facilitates the mitigation of price volatility, allowing for the acquisition of stocks at an averaged cost.

The crucial factor in executing this strategy is to guarantee that you are securing the most favorable pricing for your procurements. Certainly, it is desirable not to be the investor who consistently purchases securities at their highest market value. Engaging in such a course of action would entail allocating the utmost financial resources towards the acquisition of your stocks.

Research has incontrovertibly demonstrated that engaging in long-term investments alleviates the need for excessive apprehension, even when purchasing stocks during market peaks.

The enduring price patterns will ultimately overpower the fluctuations experienced by stocks in the minor peaks and dips occurring during short-term market volatility.

When examining technical indicators, one can observe the ability to plot moving averages on a stock chart. While the utilization of such tools may not be a concern for dividend investors, it is recommended to consider incorporating moving averages onto your stock chart to assess their visual representation. Dollar cost averaging can be conceptualized as an endeavor to purchase stocks at the price of the moving average, in the final analysis. When making regular investments in stocks, it is inevitable that you will experience instances of purchasing shares at both lower and higher prices. Given that you consistently purchase shares, the fluctuations in prices that you incur will ultimately equalize. Upon reviewing your overall purchasing activity for an extended duration such as a year, you will effectively be acquiring shares at their average price.

The greater the frequency of your stock purchases, the nearer you will come to approaching the desired average. It would be beneficial to acquire shares on a monthly basis, specifically on the 15th day. However, should you opt to acquire shares on both the 15th and 30th day of each month, that would be deemed more advantageous. If you engage in weekly stock purchases, you are further enhancing your chances. Purchasing shares on a daily basis represents the most optimal outcome. It is advisable to implement consistent intervals between each stock purchase, refraining from attempting to acquire stocks solely based on seeking bargains. The discounted price may never be promptly attainable.

Dollar cost averaging not only affects the price incurred for acquiring shares. In various scenarios, it is possible to accumulate a higher number of shares over time through the utilization of dollar cost averaging, in contrast to making one-time lump sum purchases. Instead of considering the quantity of shares to acquire, it is advisable to adopt a dollar cost averaging approach by focusing on the monetary value you intend to invest each time you purchase stocks. Occasionally, there will be instances where you will acquire a larger number of shares, while in other cases, a smaller quantity will be procured.

Establish a predetermined allocation for the acquisition of stock shares.

It is advisable to regularly purchase stocks on a monthly basis. If you choose to do so, designate a particular date upon which you consistently make stock purchases. It is imperative that you establish a rule wherein you refrain from delaying your purchase in anticipation of securing a more favorable price. You must approach this matter employing rationality and objectivity, devoid of any emotional inclinations, aspirations, or desires. Adhere to the rule under any circumstances.

If you possess the capacity to engage in more frequent stock purchasing, it would be advisable to proceed accordingly. Biweekly proves to be more advantageous than monthly, and weekly surpasses the benefits of biweekly.

Please refrain from deviating from your proposed course of action. Over the course of time, it will ultimately result in an equilibrium.

Examining a tangible illustration will demonstrate the favorability of employing dollar cost averaging, as it leads to a higher accumulation of shares. Our intention is to consider the acquisition of Facebook shares throughout a duration of one year, based on prevailing market prices. Initially, let us assume that you possess a sum of $50,000 in liquid assets, and subsequently opt to execute a singular transaction at the onset of the fiscal year. At a cost of $50,000, you will have the opportunity to acquire a total of 287 shares, assuming a share price of approximately $174 per share.

Now, let us proceed to examine a dollar cost averaging strategy. Instead of utilizing the entire sum of $50,000 in one instance, you opt for a monthly expenditure of $4,200 to acquire Facebook shares. We lack the means to predict the trajectory of the stock for the entire year; nevertheless, we are aware that the price will exhibit considerable volatility during this temporal span. Based on the factual data, the observed range of fluctuation spans from $124.95 per share to $204.87 per share. By initiating purchases consistently on the respective days of each month, with an investment amount of $4,200 per month for a duration of 12 months, the subsequent quantities could have been acquired: 24 shares, 26 shares, 27 shares, 30 shares, 34 shares, 28 shares, 26 shares, 26 shares, 24 shares, 23 shares, 22 shares, 21 shares, and ultimately 23 shares. By the conclusion of the year, our ownership would amount to a total of 334 shares. Therefore, the conclusion is that our ownership would increase by 47 shares, constituting a 16% increment in comparison to the number of shares we would have possessed if we had made a single, large-scale purchase of the stock. Envision the execution of such a stock acquisition strategy throughout a span of five, ten, or twenty years. You would ultimately acquire a substantially larger number of shares, thereby achieving a potential advantage through the equalization of share purchase prices, which could potentially result in a more favorable outcome for you. This particular instance effectively demonstrates our superior position, as our acquaintance, who made a single large purchase, was unable to capitalize on the periodic price decreases that are characteristic of any stock.

Facebook does not currently distribute a dividend; however, is it possible to consider a hypothetical scenario where it distributes a dividend of $6, comparable to IBM? The additional acquisition of 47 shares annually would result in supplementary dividend income amounting to $282. This cumulative effect, sustained over a period of 10 years, could potentially yield a substantial sum of several thousand dollars, possibly reaching an approximate figure of $3,000.

So, the concept of dollar cost averaging should not be easily disregarded. It effectively produces desirable outcomes and is poised to result in significantly improved investment performance, encompassing both the magnitude of future dividend returns and the quantity of shares currently held in your portfolio.

Indeed, it is undeniable that varying circumstances arise in different years. You are likely to encounter a scenario wherein you will be inclined to invest in securities during a period characterized by upward movement in the market. Additionally, you will inevitably encounter situations where you make stock purchases during periods of declining market movement. Ultimately, extended periods of market stagnation can be expected. In every instance, individuals may present a counterargument against dollar cost averaging, however, their standpoint will be mistaken. The aspect concerning price fluctuations is that their occurrence or direction remains uncertain to all. As a seasoned investor, you are not excessively concerned with the intricate specifics.

The practice of implementing a dollar cost averaging strategy can assist in mitigating the risk of incorrectly timing the market. This is an error that individuals frequently commit when attempting to ascertain the optimal timing for share purchases. Individuals often err in their assessments. Amidst a recent economic decline, I received input from multiple individuals cautioning me against acquiring stocks. They advised me to exercise patience as the price was expected to further decline and had not yet reached its lowest point. However, it turns out that their speculation was inaccurate. Shortly thereafter, the market experienced an upturn. I was unaware of the market's direction, yet I am indifferent to such matters. I consistently engage in regular interval purchases."

An additional advantage of dollar cost averaging lies in its ability to prevent emotional decision-making from governing your stock acquisitions. The presence of emotions in investment discussions is inherent and customary. Individuals tend to experience a state of alarm in response to declining markets, as they possess an inherent dread of potential complete financial loss. Certainly, it is an exceptionally uncommon occurrence for a company's stock to plummet to such an extent that it remains permanently unrecoverable. In nearly 99.5% of instances, stocks exhibit a post-crisis rebound, ultimately resulting in a significantly higher valuation than their pre-downturn levels in the long run.

Another manner in which emotion becomes entangled in the realm of investing is when individuals experience excessive enthusiasm and avarice upon witnessing an upward trend in stock prices.

Dollar cost averaging allows for circumvention of these challenges, as it involves systematic purchases at predetermined intervals and specified amounts. This aids in preventing the occurrence of imprudent errors. Naturally, exercising considerable self-control will be necessary to prevent succumbing to either panic or greed. However, in the event of a market decline, it is crucial to perceive it as a favorable moment to engage in purchases. Upon observing an upward trend in the market, it is imperative for one to acknowledge the reality that they are maintaining their investments for an extended duration.

This is the third advantage of dollar cost averaging, as it promotes adherence to a long-term mindset. The reaction of the markets to the most recent tweet or economic news will hold little significance in the long term, specifically in five, ten, or twenty years.

Dollar cost averaging can also serve as a strategic tool to shift your attention towards bear markets. If one comprehends the concept of dollar cost averaging and integrates it into their thought process, they will be well-equipped to commence investments in shares during significant market downturns. Allow me to suggest that you commence preparations in order to seize the opportunity of purchasing additional stocks at reduced prices. You could also allocate additional funds for this purpose. In moments of widespread distress, you can seize the opportunity to acquire additional shares at marked-down prices. This will enhance the advantages of your dollar cost averaging program.

Let us utilize the previously mentioned Facebook example as an illustration. Please be reminded that we previously encountered a circumstance in which we engaged in the purchasing of additional shares through the implementation of dollar cost averaging. As a result, our holdings increased by approximately 15-16%, equating to an additional 47 shares. There were several significant declines throughout the year; hence, what would have been the outcome if an additional sum of $4200 was invested during the most substantial decline? That could have potentially yielded us an additional 33 shares. Therefore, it would have been possible for us to conclude the fiscal year with an additional 80 shares by making an additional purchase during a period of market decline.

Downturns can prove beneficial for long-term investors, as our focus lies on the long-term trajectory spanning several decades, which typically tends to be upward. However, as investors focused on dividends, our primary objective lies in receiving consistent dividend payments through increased share ownership. Therefore, if the market maintains a predominantly horizontal trajectory from now until retirement, this would present a significantly lesser concern compared to a trader or an individual seeking to generate wealth through stock appreciation.

A potential criticism of dollar cost averaging is that as trading frequency increases, the accumulation of brokerage commissions also escalates. However, as we have witnessed, in contemporary times one has the option to register with brokerages that do not charge any fees. Therefore, the potential expenses associated with conducting trades more frequently need not be a concern.

One of the primary objections to dollar cost averaging pertains to the frequent occurrence of purchasing stocks at a relatively elevated price. However, as we have observed, it can be inferred that prices will ultimately stabilize, rendering this argument reliant on the misconception that one can accurately predict the optimal moments to purchase and sell stocks. The truth of the matter is that the day traders possess an abundance of fallacious beliefs, resulting in the majority of them experiencing financial losses. It is unattainable to accurately predict the future price movements of stocks. Could you anticipate the forthcoming instance when the President will disseminate a tweet that shall profoundly impact the financial markets? No, you are not allowed to do so - and it is impossible to anticipate a myriad of other occurrences that can influence fluctuations in prices.

Essentials

Prior to delving into more intricate concepts, I wish to furnish you with a selection of critical terminology that you will encounter throughout this book, and which is crucial for your comprehensive comprehension. Additionally, it is worth noting that I may make references to sloths, which are the lethargic and meticulous creatures commonly encountered solely through televised media. You'll understand eventually. During this interim period, we kindly request that you acquaint yourself with the following terminologies:

Shares represent fractional ownership in a corporation, entitling the holders to a portion of the company's future earnings.

Share price: a mutually determined value established between a stock seller and a stock buyer at a specific point in time, analogous to the pricing of produce at a grocery store.

Stock exchange, commonly referred to as a colloquialism, may also be denoted as an abbreviated term for an exchange. Prior to the advent of the internet, this venue served as a tangible establishment where individuals would convene for the purpose of engaging in the trade and exchange of corporate equity and various financial instruments, including bonds and commodities. Presently, these tasks can be effortlessly accomplished through online platforms, regardless of geographical limitations.

portfolio: a financial instrument that represents an individual's ownership in a trading company listed on the stock exchange, held under their name. Your investment portfolio represents the repository and documentation of the securities that you have acquired.

Mean rate of growth: the anticipated average value of an investment portfolio over time. As an illustration, suppose Diana's investment portfolio, valued at $100,000, generated a profit of $1,000 two years ago, incurred a loss of $3,000 one year ago, and is projected to yield a return of $5,000 this year. Taking these figures into account, the average growth rate of her portfolio over a span of three years can be calculated as (1% - 3% + 5%) / 3 = 1%. There will inevitably be fluctuations in her investment portfolio, yet the final value after three years demonstrates that Diana will achieve a net gain – essentially, her investment has yielded a positive average growth.

index: a comprehensive compilation of securities sharing common characteristics. There exist numerous metrics or features that delineate the index on which a company is listed. For example:

The S&P 500 index represents a compilation of the 500 most prominent publicly traded corporations that are listed on stock exchanges within the United States.

The Russell 2000 Index represents a selection of the 2,000 smallest companies among the pool of the United States' largest publicly traded companies, totaling to 3,000 in number. If you are experiencing difficulty comprehending this, that is acceptable. We shall revisit this matter at a later time.

An exchange-traded fund (ETF) refers to the consolidation of multiple securities into a single investable fund linked to a specific index. As an illustration, the Vanguard 500 Index Fund (VOO) serves as an Exchange Traded Fund (ETF) comprising a diversified portfolio of 500 carefully selected stocks, which accurately mirror the performance of the renowned S&P 500 index.

Let's Talk ETFs

What are the compelling reasons for making long-term investments in index-tracking ETFs? Mainly because it's simple. The majority of this book will guide you through the procedure of engaging in passive investing with the utilization of exchange-traded funds (ETFs), which serve as highly beneficial instruments for long-term investment strategies. It parallels the scenario wherein your maternal grandmother visits the grocery store to procure various fruits intended for a delectable fruit medley. She does not intend to purchase all of the apples. Grandmother intends to procure a variety of fruits including apples, bananas, oranges, grapes, and other assortments. — catering to a diverse range of preferences. That would be the most straightforward manner in which one could elucidate an exchange-traded fund. It retains ownership certificates of companies (i.e., shares) or certificates of debt ownership that necessitate repayment by the issuer, accompanied by interest. These financial instruments are commonly referred to as bonds.

Inquiries regarding Grandma's decision to incorporate a assortment of fruits into her fruit salad, as opposed to solely utilizing apples, would likely elicit a perplexed expression and prompt Grandma to question aloud why an individual would desire a fruit salad composed solely of apples. What are the reasons for prioritizing investment in a diversified portfolio of stocks rather than focusing on individual stocks? We will delve deeper into that explanation later in the book. Meanwhile, for the purpose of discussion, let us hypothetically consider ETFs as the most straightforward vehicle for acquiring investment knowledge and the most convenient to manage for an investor of lax inclination such as yourself.

Exchange-traded funds (ETFs) are considered highly cost-efficient investment options for individuals pursuing a passive investment strategy. It may appear complex or intricate, particularly given the fact that I am employed as an analyst within a financial services organization. Please trust my words that it is not so. I initially initiated my investments in exchange-traded funds (ETFs) during my academic years while holding a position as a security guard.

Exchange-traded funds do not function as shortcuts to financial gain. On the contrary, indeed. They represent deliberate and strategic investments undertaken with the aim of attaining sustained economic autonomy in the long run. That is the method by which we shall commence. But first...

Comprehend Your Requirements And Desires.

It seems that the words "need" and "desire" are frequently conflated by the general populace, yet in actuality, the items that individuals commonly assert as their "needs" are predominantly things they merely desire. A genuine essentiality refers to something that is indispensable for survival; without it, one's existence would ultimately cease. As an illustration, it is imperative to have sustenance and hydration. Are you familiar with the duration of time individuals can sustain without consuming water? The answer is a span of three days. What is your estimation regarding the duration for which a human being can sustain themselves without consuming food? Surprisingly, an individual can endure a period of up to fourteen days without consuming any food. Nevertheless, the majority of individuals necessitate nourishment and hydration on a daily basis.

On a daily basis, a staggering number of 4,500 children across the globe succumb to waterborne illnesses due to the consumption of contaminated water. However, it is worth noting that a significant portion of the food produced in the United States, specifically 40%, goes unconsumed. Have you ever pondered the magnitude of the quantity of human waste that exists? From an early stage of our development, it is imperative that we acquire the knowledge and skills to preserve valuable resources. That does not imply that squandering resources is acceptable solely based on our financial capacity.

Equivalent to the funds belonging to one's parents. Your parents must exert considerable effort in order to generate income. The aforementioned applies equally to those engaged in the production of food and water, as they have dedicated significant time and effort to ensure the provision of exceptional quality sustenance and unpolluted water for your consumption.

In addition, it is vital to possess appropriate attire that safeguards against the prevailing climatic conditions in your place of dwelling, be it scorching temperatures, freezing cold, or heavy precipitation. Additionally, it is imperative to secure suitable overnight accommodations that provide protection from inclement weather conditions and ensure personal safety by mitigating potential harm from malicious individuals. A shelter also serves as a facility where you can securely store commonly used possessions.

The implements and apparatus employed by individuals to earn a livelihood can be regarded as both an essentiality and a aspiration. Investing in a selection of high-grade power tools may entail a higher initial cost, yet it is imperative for the carpenter as they are utilized in daily operations. Furthermore, the superiority of these tools grants them a prolonged lifespan in comparison to their lower-cost counterparts.

On certain occasions, the maxim "good quality leads to cost-effectiveness" holds true The aforementioned illustration pertains to the notion that occasionally, investing additional funds upfront in a superior quality item can result in long-term savings, owing to its increased durability. Nevertheless, it is essential that you acquire the knowledge and skill necessary to procure a satisfactory bargain.

Apparel is an essential requirement for sustenance, however, for a significant number of individuals, a well-crafted suit remains an indulgence. It is something that they would desire to possess. In contrast, a suit serves as an essential instrument in the professional repertoire of a business executive, comparable to the indispensable tools employed by a carpenter or mechanic.

An instance is Joel's requirement to adhere to formal and elegant attire. In order to ensure durability, it is imperative that the fabric possesses a superior level of quality. Joel is required to project an authentic image, necessitating his believability and presentability, much like the exemplars provided.

Having a clear comprehension of the differentiation between necessities and desires is pivotal for achieving financial success as it grants the ability to strategize and put emphasis on one's disbursements. Alternatively, individuals should possess the capability to discern between essential necessities, indispensable requirements, and dispensable items or aspects.

Effective financial management involves the capacity to fulfill all essential "necessities," encompassing an overlooked aspect of diligently setting aside funds for future endeavors. It is imperative that you integrate this into your lifestyle. It is devoid of any semblance of desire. Simultaneously, effective financial management necessitates the possession of surplus funds that can be allocated to any preferred expenditure.

Trade Less, Make More

Buffett epitomizes the predominant philosophy of minimal trading and long-term investment in the financial world. He holds an intensely strong aversion towards short-term trading, to the extent that he once humorously proposed a radical alteration in tax legislation that would impose a 100% tax on gains derived from trades executed within a year. It seems that the shareholders of Berkshire Hathaway have understood the message conveyed by Mr. Buffett. Therefore, the level of share turnover in Berkshire is notably minimal, to the extent that certain shareholders choose to pass down their shares to future generations in order to prevent their descendants from selling them in the future.

Envision a scenario where your investment choices are conveyed through a limited punchcard, symbolizing a mere twenty allocations, each possessing implications for a lifetime. Each investment decision made leads to the depletion of one card from your lifetime allocation. By reserving them for exceptional ideas, you will never exhaust all 20 opportunities."

Although it may appear somewhat impractical, adopting this perspective can be beneficial when considering your investment choices.

If one lacks the commitment to maintain ownership of a stock for a decade, it would be ill-advised to entertain the notion of holding it for a mere ten minutes.

Prestigious academician, Prem Jain, who holds the distinguished position of Professor at the Georgetown University McDonough School of Business and authored the enlightening book titled Buffett Beyond Value: Why Buffett Looks to Growth and Management When Investing, made an astute observation regarding Buffett's distinctive perspective. Jain remarked, 'In a milieu where the majority tend to prioritize short-term interests, adopting a far-reaching outlook confers exceptional benefits.' "When the collective influence of short-term investors affects market dynamics, long-term investors who possess a strong sense of independent thinking have the opportunity to counteract and ultimately achieve exceptional profits." Buffett's ability to exhibit patience serves as a crucial attribute that defines his investment strategy and disposition. He is prepared to patiently bide his time, harboring abundant financial resources until an ideal investment opportunity arises. This can entail persevering through challenging periods of observing the market surge to unprecedented levels, while you remain on the figurative periphery, anticipating the opportune moment when promising enterprises achieve a more equitable valuation, simultaneously witnessing the depreciation of your accumulated funds as they struggle to match the escalating inflation. Nevertheless, it is imperative that you possess the fortitude to undertake this endeavor.

Buffett has occasionally experienced missteps in the course of his career, making investments in companies that did not meet his customary standards due to limited opportunities, and on each occasion, he subsequently expressed remorse (acknowledging his fallibility as a human being). An infamous instance of this can be seen in the case of US Airways, wherein Berkshire made an investment in the year 1989. On occasion, each of us is susceptible to committing errors of this nature. However, once you encounter these failures, make a conscious effort to glean valuable lessons from them and proceed forward, mirroring the tenacity and resilience demonstrated by Buffett. Please refrain from being overly critical of yourself, instead, direct your attention towards acquiring the skill of patience, remaining stationary, and awaiting a favorable market condition that would justify investing your diligently earned money into a company. As articulated by Mr. Buffett during Berkshire's annual meeting in 1998, amidst the reproach for his lack of involvement in the market's upswing, he declared, "We shall not engage in acquiring assets indiscriminately merely to fulfill a quota. We exclusively make purchases when we perceive them to be appealing...compensation is not provided for mere engagement. One earns a salary by being correct."

Buffett often emphasizes the importance of patiently awaiting the opportune moment, referred to as the 'fat pitch', which enables investors to exercise the freedom of avoiding costly errors. In his interview with the New York Times in 2007, he elucidated his thought process by stating, "A desirable aspect of investing is that one need not hastily make decisions and can selectively choose opportunities." One has the ability to observe pitches arriving slightly above or below the level of one's navel, without necessarily engaging in a swinging motion. No official arbiter will deem you as out. You are free to exercise patience in anticipation of the desired investment opportunity. As investors, we possess the privilege of awaiting favorable conditions, with no external pressure save for our own internal impatience, which we can strive to manage effectively. We diverge from baseball players who constantly face the burden of expectations from both their coaches and fans, compelling them to swing. It is advisable to refrain from hasty decisions of intervention upon observing an increase in stock values, particularly influenced by unsubstantiated financial information and sensationalized opinions. Buffett demonstrated remarkable patience over the course of multiple years, refraining from deploying approximately $44 billion in cash that remained unutilized on Berkshire's balance sheet from 2004 to 2007.

Subsequently, as the market experienced a significant decline in the autumn of 2008 amidst the financial crisis, he identified a favorable investment opportunity and swiftly capitalized on it by deploying $20 billion towards the acquisition of Goldman Sachs and General Electric stocks. His conduct provides motivation for others to surmount apprehension and alarm, and seize the ample prospects the market was affording them during that period. As he frequently emphasizes, in one of his most renowned and captivating expressions, "Exhibit voracity amidst others' trepidation, and trepidation amidst others' voracity." Furthermore, exhibiting patience is of paramount importance subsequent to undertaking an investment in a corporation. On occasion, unforeseen circumstances arise wherein immediately subsequent to your acquisition of stock, it undergoes a decline in value. Every investor will inevitably experience this at least once, causing immediate questioning of one's decision-making process. It is possible that the market is experiencing a significant downturn, or alternatively, it appears that your specific investment has failed to realize the intended increase in value, thus deviating from its intended trajectory.

Nevertheless, it can be exceedingly dispiriting to witness what one was confident would transpire as an unequivocal certainty ultimately unfold in a seemingly contrasting manner. However, one must not succumb to panic and hastily engage in the act of selling. If you diligently complete your assignments and remain steadfast in your investment beliefs, you must persevere. It is imperative that you exercise patience and refrain from succumbing to the temptation of compromising any opportunity for sustained success. Buffett encountered a comparable circumstance when Berkshire initiated the acquisition of shares in the Washington Post company in 1973. Immediately, in the midst of a tumultuous bearish market, second in severity only to the one experienced in

2008, the stock experienced a precipitous 20% decline, maintaining this low level until 1976. It was not until 1981 that the valuation of the Washington Post reached the level deemed appropriate by Warren Buffett. Buffett has retained ownership of his shares in the post throughout periods of economic decline, subsequent recoveries, and several presidential administrations, establishing it as one of his most profitable investments to date. This position can be regarded as a fundamental, long-term holding that Buffett has no plans to divest, intending it to remain within Berkshire's portfolio indefinitely.

Had he chosen to withdraw at the initial indication of market upheaval, he would have forgone the opportunity to partake in a substantial victory. Exercising restraint can at times cause discomfort, but ultimately, the rewards outweigh the temporary hardship. Achieving success as an investor presents significant challenges. It necessitates courage, resilience, readiness, and a commitment to refrain from taking action merely for the purpose of appearing active.

The Functioning Of The Stock Market

Upon acquiring the skill of driving, you did not simply initiate the vehicle by entering and starting it instantly. Conversely, an individual provided meticulous guidance on the necessary procedures prior to your commencement of vehicle operation. You were previously informed about the purpose and functionality of both the stick-shift and automatic gear selector, commonly referred to as PRNDL. You were instructed on the procedure for adjusting the mirrors, distinguishing between forward and reverse, as well as operating the various controls within the vehicle. Prior to making any investments in the stock market, it is important to proceed with caution rather than haste. You require a comprehensive instructional resource that provides insight into operational procedures, ensuring the prevention of financially burdensome errors. Provided that one possesses a deep understanding of the mechanics, there should be no cause for trepidation when confronted with the actuality of a given circumstance. A significant number of individuals lack comprehension of investment strategies, thus causing them to experience apprehension when it comes to engaging with the stock market. The truth of the matter is that acquiring an understanding of its functioning and the constituent components will enable you to formulate an investment strategy that proves effective.

Typically, a stock is commonly denoted as a share. It represents an ownership stake in a corporation actively seeking investment opportunities. These investors contribute financial resources to support the company's expansion and development. When a corporation initially issues shares to the public, it is commonly referred to as an IPO, which stands for Initial Public Offering. The valuation of the company, along with the quantity of shares being offered, determines the share price.

In order for the shares to be made available to the general public, it is necessary for the company to become listed on a recognized stock exchange such as the New York Stock Exchange (NYSE). Subsequently, traders and investors are able to engage in the purchasing and selling of stocks, yet the company shall solely accrue profits through the initial public offering. Following the conclusion of the initial public offering (IPO), the subsequent trading of stocks primarily involves the engagement of business professionals, individuals, and investors who conduct transactions amongst one another with the intention of generating financial gains and acquiring dividend payouts.

Investing in equities through the stock exchange

Investors and traders divest from stocks post-IPO with regard to the perceived valuation. The value of a corporation has the potential to appreciate or decline, presenting an opportunity for investors to generate profits. An increase in the stock price of a company can lead to a profitable return. In the event that an investor acquires said shares and experiences a decline in price or company valuation, monetary loss will be incurred by the investor. It is equally the investors and traders who will influence the price movement, whether in an upward or downward trajectory.

Investors possess either of two objectives: to make short-term or long-term investments. A long-term investment relies on the expectation that a stock will sustain an upward trajectory in its price. A brief duration investment entails the objective of swiftly acquiring capital, while promptly withdrawing prior to any decline in the stock's value.

Established corporations provide regular dividend payments to their stockholders. If one possesses shares, it implies their status as a shareholder in a given company. If an investor retains stocks for a considerable duration and possesses a significant stake in a company, they gain the prerogative to participate in the election of new members of the board. Dividends refer to the portion of a company's profits that is distributed among its shareholders.

Investors stand to gain monetary returns from both the variations in prices and the dividends. A seller frequently endeavors to generate earnings through the sale made to a prospective buyer. The prospective purchaser is also seeking to acquire the assets at the lowest possible price, anticipating that as the stock price continues to rise, they will yield a profit.

The profitability of the investment is determined by subtracting the initial purchase price from the closing or selling price. As an illustration, the purchase of Google shares at a price of $400, followed by an increase in value to $600, would result in a per-share profit of $200.

Sellers have the ability to decrease the price as a result of the forces of supply and demand. The functionality of this financial market operates on the basis of the interplay between supply and demand.

Disadvantages of Penny Stock

To ensure equitable, impartial, and astute decisions, one must thoroughly consider the disadvantages. This holds particular significance in terms of equipping you and counteracting the potential drawbacks, if they were to manifest. Possessing the capacity to enhance the benefits and mitigate the risks through strategic countermeasures is an unequivocal approach to fostering one's triumph.

Having knowledge about the potential danger can also assist you in steering clear of it. Ultimately, during the expedition through the jungle in search of the treasure, possessing a comprehensive understanding of the perils at hand will undoubtedly prove advantageous. Acquiring the skill of minimizing potential risks is crucial for achieving success in trading penny stocks. Moreover, developing the ability to endure losses and bounce back is even more advantageous. It can be likened to honing the capacity to withstand financial downturns within the realm of investing. Regrettably, few individuals possess the necessary skills to effectively manage financial adversity. The majority of the companies possessing penny stocks tend to exhibit lower quality attributes. Consequently, the potential implications suggest that both the reputation and sales may experience limited advancement or, alternatively, could succumb to excessive strain. Hence, a comprehensive investigation into the company's caliber and strategic roadmap becomes imperative. If it fails to adapt or withstand the intensity of competition, that is a significant cause for concern. Furthermore, it should be noted that organizations burdened with significant debt are unquestionably regarded as a significant cause for concern.

Despite people's reluctance to acknowledge it, a significant majority of investors ultimately incur financial losses. This is primarily due to their involvement in volatile markets that lack substantial regulatory oversight. This enables enterprises to operate under disparate regulations, thereby frequently resulting in more adverse consequences. It is highly improbable to exit penny stock trading without incurring some degree of financial detriment. You are required to adequately prepare for this situation and demonstrate self-compassion in the event of a loss.

While it is not entirely devoid of regulations, it implies that it operates under distinct guidelines. If you aspire to make investments in penny stocks, it will be necessary for you to acquire comprehensive knowledge of the various regulatory frameworks pertaining to penny stocks. It is crucial to bear in mind that the application of investment methods, strategies, and regulations for penny stocks differs significantly from those employed for conventional stocks. Operating under a distinct set of principles entails a heightened capacity to adjust and engage in innovative thinking. If simplicity is a desired outcome, it may be prudent to pursue long-term, large-scale investments.

Additionally, there exists a diminished level of trading activity, wherein the trading of penny stocks occurs with limited market participation. This implies that the frequency of transactions is either higher or lower than the average volume of stocks, necessitating astute decision-making. In conjunction with this, there is a notable presence of elevated volatility, which heightens the potential for potential financial losses if one is not cautious; however, it should be noted that volatility within the realm of penny stock trading is not necessarily entirely detrimental. It could indicate an elevated level of risk; however, in due course, you will become acquainted with the favorable attributes of the volatility that can be harnessed to generate profits.

Furthermore, this phenomenon poses a significant risk across the entire spectrum of stocks and shares within the financial domain. However, due to the inherent characteristics of penny stocks, the likelihood of encountering fraudulent activities in this specific category is notably higher. Due to the dearth of information and a reduction in regulatory measures, the establishment of fraudulent schemes becomes more convenient, necessitating a perpetual state of vigilance to mitigate potential risks. Frequently encountered schemes in the market include the practice of pump and dump, wherein stock promoters swiftly bolster the stock's value by making substantial personal investments and promoting the inflated price through social media channels. Subsequently, after the price escalates to an overstated extent, they proceed to divest their stocks, leaving investors with virtually no capital remaining.

Another frequently encountered challenge associated with trading penny stocks is the additional charges imposed in the form of commission fees. It is important to note that while the majority of brokerages maintain reasonable commission rates, penny stocks unfortunately serve as an exception to this. Penny stocks incur significantly higher commission charges, necessitating careful scrutiny of the associated fees prior to enrolling in any transactions. It would be regrettable if any profits you may generate were to be diminished by fees, or even worse, if you were to incur losses. Regrettably, the inclusion of commission fees is an inherent aspect of engaging with an intermediary and can impede your advancement in dealings involving inexpensive stocks. Once more, please ensure that you are utilizing the appropriate platform and remain informed regarding any applicable commission charges. Refrain from engaging in unnecessary trades that may result in excessive commission fees; instead, exercise greater caution in your decision-making process and diligently monitor the associated fees. They will accumulate gradually and can significantly impede your progress if you do not exercise caution.

Nevertheless, this should not be the sole portrayal of penny trading that you encounter. There exists a multitude of factors beyond the purview of a rifle scope that contribute significantly to the game. However, the insights facilitated by the aforementioned tool provide an excellent foundation upon which to formulate an equitable and impartial judgement. The phenomenon of penny stock investments similarly illustrates the concept that a story or situation can possess multiple perspectives. Many of these risks can be mitigated, or if encountered, effectively managed to minimize their impact. It can also provide unequivocal insight into whether you possess the aptitude for penny stock trading, as both day trading and penny stock trading are indisputably unsuitable for all individuals. Ensure that you are adequately motivated and prepared for the undertaking at hand, as it is of considerable magnitude.

Numerous anecdotes exist regarding the achievements of individuals engaging in the field of penny stocks. Despite the significant risks involved, the potential rewards are equally substantial. Upon conducting an investigation into their narratives, nevertheless, it becomes evident that they indeed possess a wealth of experience, having built their success through perseverance, learning from errors, unwavering commitment, and an astute understanding of the respective market they operate within. Regrettably, acquiring substantial wealth proves to be a challenge, and hence, this disheartening truth often causes individuals to relinquish their pursuits in the realm of investment.

This may prompt inquiry regarding the following: Is it possible to genuinely generate a substantial income through the buying and selling of penny stocks? Regrettably, absolute assurance cannot be provided to you, as the market's unpredictability prevents anyone from possessing the capacity to accurately foresee its outcomes (otherwise, individuals would have achieved significantly higher levels of success).

Trading may not pose formidable challenges; however, a considerable number of individuals fail to acquire the requisite expertise for achieving success in this endeavor. Adequate research and diligent effort can effectively mitigate numerous drawbacks mentioned. Therefore, in response to your inquiry, it is imperative to acknowledge that without sufficient knowledge or understanding of the mechanics behind penny stocks, one would not possess the necessary groundwork to attain success.

Fundamentally, one has the capacity to generate income. You possess the capacity to. However, diligent efforts, self-control, and strategic maneuvers can undeniably enhance your prospects. Naturally, the occurrence of trial and error is inevitable, yet it decidedly remains a certainty within the realm of trading. Mistakes are a common occurrence amongst us all, and those who derive wisdom from them exhibit great sagacity.

Engaging in penny stock trading is not a pursuit suited for individuals seeking effortless endeavors; rather, it appeals to those who possess a desire to acquire knowledge and understanding. It entails a substantial procedure and necessitates thorough contemplation of various factors. In order to distinguish oneself from the masses, one must exert additional endeavor.

More troubling is the fact that distinguishing oneself from the majority is not particularly arduous, as the majority lacks the inclination to invest the necessary time and effort. Consequently, I would highly advise you to invest valuable time and exert significant effort to distinguish yourself from others.

Avatars Serve As A Representation Of Our Digital Persona.

Fundamentally, the coherence and meaningfulness of all online activities, such as accessing videos or browsing images on platforms like Google or Instagram, rely solely upon their association with a particular individual. A wallet does not serve as an optimal means to visually epitomize one's identity, rather it is an Avatar.

A cryptographic avatar shall be employed as a symbol of individuals within the realm of virtual reality. These avatars establish a distinctive digital persona in terms of visual embodiment within the realm of virtual reality – they serve as your delegate in the metaverse. The Avatar serves as the focal point through which users articulate their self-expression. It imparts individuals with insights into your identity. It is more convenient to retain in memory an aesthetically pleasing or unconventional avatar, as opposed to recalling a cryptographic username or wallet.

Nevertheless, you are limited to utilizing a single Avatar in any given location.

Strategies for establishing a novel digital persona within the metaverse.

Crypto Avatar is a comprehensive platform that empowers users to fabricate and subsequently distribute their personalized Avatar, effectively rendering it accessible for integration across diverse applications. There exists a method by which you can incorporate your 3D character creation into these platforms for crypto avatars. While engaged in the process of avatar creation, it is imperative to meticulously ensure that the end product aligns with the designated specifications. In order to utilize select avatars within VR chat, it is imperative to ensure that the mesh comprises no more than 7500 triangles.

Please ensure that your Avatar possesses anthropomorphic characteristics, consisting of two limbs, two appendages, and a cranial region. Utilize a 3D computer application or employ mixamo graphics technology software to generate this Avatar. Provided that you possess a valid Adobe license, you will be able to utilize this software. In order to incorporate facial animations to all the avatars you have created, you will need to utilize blendshapes.

The primary step in establishing a fresh identity is to commence the creation of an FBX file.

Utilize the blender software to generate a three-dimensional character. Position the limbs, torso, and head in a forward direction. Devote sufficient time to acquire the necessary skills for crafting characters.

Please ensure that you include a mesh, a rig, and blend shapes when exporting the characters from the blender.

It is imperative to bear in mind that the characters possess a finite limit of 7,500 polygons.

Please locate the 'file manager' and proceed to select 'export selection.' Then, navigate to the 'export as FBX' option and ensure that all animations and models are chosen. Finally, select 'centimeters' as the units and save the file in the fbx format.

Following that, proceed to import the fbx file into the Unity software.

Guidelines for importing fbx files into the Unity platform

● To begin, please proceed with the installation of the unity application on your system. Develop a new project utilizing the most recent version of Unity.

● Seek out the VRM software development kit and proceed with its download. Please make sure you obtain the unity package. Once you have successfully downloaded it, proceed to drag and drop each individual item into the Unity interface. Upon successful installation, a folder will become visible in the virtual reality module (VRM), accompanied by the presence of a menu option within the tool's menu at the uppermost section.

● Generate a novel directory within this unity application, proceed to relocate and integrate the FBX avatar into the designated directory. Subsequently, proceed to import the files and verify that they are set to a standard map mode.

● To initiate the process, perform a right-click using your mouse, proceed to the 'create' option, followed by selecting 'material.' Then, transfer and release the textures into the primary map field.

● Upon completing this action, your Avatar will be prepared for creation. Please ensure that you click on the 'mesh file,' then proceed to select the 'rig' and opt for 'humanoid' as the animation type in your drop-down menu. Initiate the application process and preserve the scene while awaiting the rig's configuration.

● Upon reaching this stage, ensure that the character's ligaments correspond accurately with the designated label. The leg situated in the top left quadrant should be correctly identified as the intended left leg in an elevated position.

● Upon completion, return to your scene menu, navigate to the 'mesh' option, and locate the VRM menu at the top. Please designate the UniVRM option from the dropdown menu and proceed to select the 'export humanoid' function.

• Please input your information, select either the option labeled 'force T-pose' or the option labeled 'pose freeze,' and utilize the 'experimental export' functionality. Subsequently, transfer these files to the specific directory located alongside your remaining files. The recently added folders will be displayed within the designated project section.

• Subsequently, remove the mesh from the scene menu and proceed to place your pre-can into the scene. There will be a T-pose present.

• Next, opt for the mesh, navigate to the VRM section, specifically choose the UniVRM option, and proceed to export your humanoid model. Please verify whether the options for freezing the pose, selecting T-pose, and enabling experimental export have been deselected. Next, select the option labeled 'export.' Proceed by tapping on the 'export' button.

Please proceed with the exportation of the VRM file. Please be advised that there is a possibility of the Avatar not being fully compatible with your VR chat experience. There are numerous processes involved in arranging it, and crypto Avatars offer comprehensive guidance (documentation) on its execution.

Varieties of virtual reality" "Classifications of virtual reality" "Categories of virtual reality" "Forms of virtual reality

There exists a variety of virtual reality technologies. Annually, technology firms unveil their iterations of virtual reality. Here is a compilation of the different types of virtual reality.

Non- immersive reality

The absence of immersion can be observed in the virtual reality flight simulator. The personal computer is equipped with an expansive widescreen display and is accompanied by a comprehensive peripheral system, encompassing various accessories such as joysticks, headsets, and more. The term "non-immersive reality" is used to describe this phenomenon as it refers to the situation where users do not become fully immersed in the virtual reality experience generated by the device. It fails to provide the user with an immersive gaming experience. It is nearly akin to merely observing the game on the display. The level of engagement in the game is limited or insufficient; while you will still encounter virtual reality, it lacks depth and immersion.

Fully immersive reality

The complete immersion into reality is achieved through the utilization of a highly advanced virtual reality system, powered by a robust computer. The robust computational system possesses the capability to perceive visual stimuli, auditory signals, and even subtle movements. One should possess the capability to modify the user's experience. The individual equipped with a head-mounted display and sensory gloves will be able to partake in a highly immersive virtual reality experience. In order to obtain an immersive virtual reality experience, it will be necessary to utilize a pair of monitors.

The augmented reality

Augmented reality bears resemblance to the virtual reality encounter, as it operates at the intersection of the tangible reality and the digital realm. Primarily, it entails an immersion in the veracity of our surroundings. For instance, consider a scenario wherein an individual seeks information on a historical landmark through online sources. Under such circumstances, certain mappings offer 3D functionalities that render the landmarks, historical sites, structures, and relevant informational details to the individual. One may utilize their computer to explore captivating historical sites via their smartphone. Enhanced reality enables users to experience a three-dimensional perspective by leveraging their mobile devices, thereby immersing themselves in a virtual realm within the physical environment.

Web-based

One can engage in various virtual reality games accessible through the utilization of the virtual reality markup language (VRML) by means of the internet. This facilitates individuals to explore novel and captivating offerings of the internet service. Individuals can engage in meaningful and enjoyable interactions with their loved ones and acquaintances through social media.

The collaborative reality

Collaborative reality bears significant resemblance to virtual reality games, yet it lacks the immersive qualities typically associated with them. Virtual reality provides the viewer with an interactive and immersive experience facilitating communication. This feature will facilitate the sharing of your experience with other individuals in the digital realm.

Method Twelve: Dog Walking

If you are contemplating a vocation that involves dedicating your time to interacting with canines and earning a living, the profession of a dog walker could be a suitable choice to ponder upon. Engaging in dog walking can provide an exceptional physical activity, particularly for individuals who possess an affinity towards enjoying the outdoors.

One notable drawback entails the responsibility of tending to post-elimination cleanup following the activities of domesticated animals. It is rather disconcerting when individuals demonstrate reluctance to collaborate or when one is subjected to adverse outdoor conditions. Once you have carefully assessed the advantages and disadvantages of pursuing this profession, and provided that you have confidence in your abilities as a dog walker, you must adequately prepare yourself.

During the job interview process, it is commonplace for companies, applications, and potential employers to inquire about your level of expertise and experience in handling and caring for dogs. In order to demonstrate your competence with canines, certain individuals may consider a substantial background in dog ownership acceptable, whereas others may require additional substantiation of your proficiency in handling dogs.

To enhance your chances of securing employment as a dog walker, you may want to inquire with your relatives and acquaintances about the possibility of offering your dog walking services to them and whether they would be willing to serve as references for your future applications. To commence, it is imperative that you initiate:

One should not make the assumption that possessing or having owned a dog in the past automatically equips them with the complete knowledge necessary. Certain dogs may experience difficulty in walking due to their inherent character traits. You will have the opportunity to collaborate with various breeds of dogs, making it of utmost importance to possess expertise in this domain.

To achieve success, one must possess these attributes.

Ensure that you consistently demonstrate care, compassion, and regard towards your prospective clients (dogs) throughout your interactions with them.

Compassion is crucial when interacting with animals. In the first place, it is imperative for one to establish a rapport with the animals, fostering an environment where familiarity is cultivated from both ends.

To cultivate customer loyalty, it is imperative to ensure that your clientele is consistently satisfied and content with the quality of your services.

The client's assessment of your reliability greatly depends on your unwavering dedication to punctuality during the walking sessions.

In the event that a canine exhibits pulling behavior, it is imperative to possess the necessary physical stamina to effectively manage the dog while ensuring continued control over the leash. Furthermore, it is imperative that you possess the ability to engage in continuous walking for a minimum duration of thirty minutes.

The following are the tasks that will be assigned to you-

Furnish the pets with exercise sessions, typically lasting for durations of thirty minutes to one hour.

Kindly collect and dispose of any excrement while walking the canine.

Ensure that the canine is adequately nourished and hydrated prior to embarking on a stroll.

Please promptly notify any issues regarding the health of dogs and seek immediate medical assistance should their condition deteriorate.

It is imperative for dog walkers to ensure the safety of their clients' pets during the course of their walks. To ensure appropriate contact information is readily available in case of emergencies, pet owners are typically mandated to complete a form containing their contact details, the contact information of the pet's veterinarian, as well as pertinent information such as the pet's weight, age, breed, medical conditions, and prescribed medications.

Certain individuals engaged in dog walking work independently, whereas others undertake their activities within the framework of a company they either own or manage, thus enlisting the services of additional dog walkers. The service has the potential to accommodate a larger customer base and extend its coverage area. In addition, certain pet walkers also offer pet sitting and grooming services.

TIP

The standard remuneration for walking a dog amounts to an average of $17 per session, whereas if an individual possesses considerable expertise in this field, they may be able to command a fee of $20.

Key Points

In the present chapter, we have addressed the range of activities encompassing the seventh through twelfth tasks pertaining to income generation. Prior to progressing further, let us encapsulate the salient aspects.

One can acquire a source of income by acquiring the skill of selling on the Amazon platform.

An alternative internet-based platform for marketing and selling your merchandise is eBay.

One can engage in the production and marketing of lemonade, especially during the scorching summer period.

One could engage in the production and marketing of cupcakes, or alternatively, organize a designated day for the sale of baked goods.

You can walk dogs.

In the subsequent chapter, we shall delve into an additional six alternatives for gaining monetary resources and augmenting one's way of life.

Advantages And Disadvantages Of Passive Funds

Having gained a comprehensive understanding of active management funds, our primary focus within this book shall be directed towards passive investment funds. Upholding a well-balanced portfolio is a crucial investment tactic and the bedrock for passive funds. Index funds are a passive investment strategy that achieves diversification through the dispersion of risk. They achieve this by maintaining a substantial portfolio of securities within their benchmark. Such funds are designed to align with a specific benchmark or index, with no objective of actively identifying successful investment opportunities. By adopting this approach, they are able to mitigate the need for constant buying and selling of securities. Consequently, they exhibit reduced fees and expenses compared to funds managed actively. Active funds necessitate diligent monitoring by a manager, whereas passive investments such as index funds exhibit tracking capabilities, making them a straightforward avenue for investment in a preferred market.

In addition to the exceptionally low fees and diminished risks associated with investing in passive funds, there exist a multitude of other advantages. In the first instance, a notable aspect pertains to the high level of transparency, ensuring that you are continually apprised of the specific assets that are implicated. The buy-and-hold strategy generally does not lead to substantial capital gains taxes throughout the year. In conclusion, the possession of an index fund or a collection of indices is significantly more convenient and requires less effort compared to an actively managed fund. In the context of an actively managed fund, a significant amount of strategic decision-making is involved, necessitating continuous research and adaptation. If one fails to allocate due attention to an actively managed fund over a period of time, they may suffer significant financial losses. This is unlikely to transpire in a passive fund due to the absence of necessity for active participation.

Similar to any positive aspect, passive funds also possess their drawbacks. It would be advisable for you to familiarize yourself with these details in order to be adequately informed. In general, advocates of active funds commonly express the following criticisms regarding passive funds.

They possess excessively restrictive parameters. Passive funds adhere to a pre-established selection of investments, with a minimal scope for deviation. This implies that investors are bound to retain their investments regardless of the market's fluctuations. The significant absence of adaptability greatly discourages proactive investors. They are effectively bound to stocks, even in instances where their performance is subpar. If other stocks within their index are performing favorably, these losses can be counterbalanced.

Their potential returns are comparatively lower. By virtue of their inherent characteristics, passive funds will always fall short of outperforming the market. Despite significant market turbulence, their holdings remain steadfastly aligned with market movements. The sole instance in which a significant return will ensue is when the market experiences a substantial surge. However, it will be significantly overshadowed by actively managed funds.

Index funds are widely regarded as being highly suitable for diverse retirement accounts such as 401ks or IRAs. Respected investor Warren Buffett characterizes them as a sanctuary for accumulating funds intended for one's later stages in life. The majority of individuals do not engage in investment activities on a full-time basis. They are employed in conventional occupations, engaged in nurturing familial relationships, pursuing leisure activities and other areas of personal fascination, thereby allocating the bulk of their time. They might lack the capacity to engage in aggressive investment strategies. In light of this perspective, index funds and other passive investment strategies appear to be more rational. It facilitates the opportunity for individuals of ordinary means to acquire stocks across diverse companies at a modest expense, subsequently yielding favorable returns over an extended duration.

By establishing a retirement account during the early stages of your life and consistently allocating a specific portion of your savings, there exists the possibility of accumulating substantial wealth, reaching the range of hundreds of thousands or even millions, as you approach the designated retirement phase. Naturally, this outcome is contingent on the extent of your investment and the market's performance. Purchasing shares in a specific corporation significantly enhances the likelihood of experiencing favorable returns over a span of 40 years, as opposed to a relatively short duration of one or two years. Once an individual initiates the establishment of a passive fund investment account, it is advisable to allocate a specific portion of their earnings to be regularly contributed on a monthly basis. Please refrain from withdrawing the funds until your retirement, unless there is a significant emergency warranting such action.

The objective when introducing diversification into an index fund is to replicate a specific "index," encompassing either the entire stock market or a specific segment of it, through a wide range of holdings. The fund will subsequently replicate the index's performance. There is an index fund available for virtually every financial market across the globe. The United States possesses multiple indices, with the S&P 500 being the most widely recognized and utilized among them. Additional significant indices comprise the Dow Jones Industrial Average, Nasdaq Composite, Barclays, and Willshire 5,000 Total Market Index, among various others. An index fund designed to track the Dow Jones would allocate investments in the very same companies that make up this specific index. The index could possibly employ a weighting methodology, resulting in a greater allocation of funds towards specific securities relative to others. From time to time, a portfolio manager can assist in the restructuring and rebalancing of these proportions.

A Comprehensive Guide To Acquiring Cryptocurrency: The Process Of Bitcoin Acquisition

By dissecting the procedural complexities of investing in Bitcoin (BTCUSD) into attainable segments, the task becomes considerably more straightforward.

Thorough Preparation Is imperative Prior to Engaging in Bitcoin Investments. A valid form of personal identification (when working with a KYC platform) and access to the internet are indispensable for individuals aspiring to engage with the Bitcoin community. It is recommended to possess an individual wallet distinct from your exchange account as well. This method facilitates payments through the utilization of bank accounts, debit cards, and credit cards. Bitcoin can also be acquired through dedicated automated teller machines (ATMs) and by utilizing peer-to-peer

(P2P) platforms. Nevertheless, as of the commencement of the year 2020, Bitcoin ATMs have instituted a prerequisite for the presentation of official identification documents provided by the government.

Bitcoin investors have expressed apprehension with regards to the confidentiality and safeguarding of their financial activities.

Anyone in possession of the private key corresponding to a public address on the blockchain has the authority to authorize Bitcoin transactions. If individuals with malicious intent discover that you possess a substantial amount of monetary value, they may endeavor to abscond with your confidential access codes. Please bear in mind that a public speech's equilibrium may be observed by all who have the opportunity to listen to it. Consequently, due to the availability of this public information, individuals possess the opportunity to establish numerous public aliases. Consequently, they possess the capability to distribute their Bitcoins among a vast array of addresses. Public addresses that remain unutilized for transactions present an attractive opportunity for substantial investments.

The transaction history of a blockchain is accessible to all individuals, including the account holder. In spite of the presence of transaction logs on the blockchain, the identification of specific users remains unattainable. In order to maintain transaction confidentiality while preserving traceability, the Bitcoin blockchain exclusively reveals the public key of individuals participating in the transaction. Due to the fact that Bitcoin transactions are visible to any observer, they possess a higher level of transparency and traceability compared to confidential cash transactions. In contrast, Bitcoin transactions possess a certain level of anonymity. In the bitcoin blockchain, discerning the identities of individuals participating in a transaction, including both the sender and recipient, presents a formidable challenge.

According to experts from worldwide sources and the Federal Bureau of Investigation (FBI), it is possible to establish connections between transactions conducted on the Bitcoin blockchain and various online accounts, such as digital wallets.

An individual seeking to initiate an account with Coinbase will be required to provide documentation verifying their identity. Subsequently, each time that person makes a purchase of Bitcoin, it becomes associated with their personal information. The account holder's identity remains associated with the

Coinbase purchase, even in the event of transferring the cryptocurrency to a different wallet. The legality of Bitcoin in the United States and numerous other developed countries should serve to reassure the majority of investors.

6.1 Procurement of Bitcoin

We have provided a comprehensive breakdown of the bitcoin purchasing procedure below. It is important to bear in mind that conducting independent research remains necessary and imperative to selecting the optimal solution for your particular circumstances.

6.1.1 Select a Cryptocurrency Trading Service or Platform

Prior to acquiring bitcoins, it is necessary for you to select a cryptocurrency trading provider or platform. Cryptocurrency exchanges, payment service providers, and financial brokerages represent prominent platforms for the acquisition of digital assets. This option is particularly advantageous as it offers an extensive array of features and a larger selection of tradable currencies compared to other platforms.

If you opt to engage in a cryptocurrency exchange, you will have the opportunity to engage in the buying, selling, and safekeeping of various cryptocurrencies. It is often advisable to engage in an exchange that allows consumers to transfer their digital currency to their personal online wallet as a means of safeguarding their assets. This feature may not hold significant relevance for individuals seeking to engage in Bitcoin or other cryptocurrency trading.

There exists a broad array of bitcoin exchanges that are accessible for utilization. In order to uphold principles of decentralization and individual liberty, certain exchanges do not necessitate the submission of personal details from users and do not rely on the concept of anonymity. Consequently, these exchanges lack a singular point of control and operate autonomously.

Such systems have the potential to be advantageous for the global population lacking access to banking services, albeit with the acknowledgment that they may be susceptible to misuse. Anonymous transactions could prove beneficial to specific demographics, such as individuals in refugee situations or those residing in nations lacking substantial or non-existent credit or banking systems.

Nevertheless, the majority of the prevailing exchanges lack decentralization and necessitate users to furnish identification documents during the registration procedure. Coinbase, Kraken, Gemini, FTX.US, and Binance.US represent a select number of the numerous cryptocurrency exchanges operating within the United States, catering to American users in the present day. Ever since the commencement of these exchanges, there has been a remarkable surge in the range of products and services they provide.

In recent years, there has been a proliferation of new tokens, each vying for the attention and investment of participants in the cryptocurrency market. Certain virtual currencies, such as Bitcoin and Ethereum, can only be accessed through a limited number of exchanges. Each exchange employs a multitude of criteria to assess the eligibility of a specific token for trading on its platform.

One can potentially purchase bitcoin on these three exchanges, which additionally offer an expanding range of alternative cryptocurrencies, such as Ethereum and Ripple. These three cryptocurrency entry points are potentially the most accessible and user-friendly among all industry options. Binance caters to the more adept trader, offering sophisticated trading functionalities and an extensive range of alternative cryptocurrencies to select from. The FTX crypto market offers a restricted selection of cryptocurrencies for trading to US investors. 2

However, the platform offers a greater selection of tokens for traders residing outside the United States.

When establishing a bitcoin exchange account, it is imperative to adhere to prudent online security measures. For the purpose of two-factor authentication, it is imperative to utilize a password that is both distinctive and lengthy, encompassing a diverse array of lowercase and uppercase letters, special characters, as well as numerals.

Strategies For Investing In Precious Metals

Over the course of numerous millennia, valuable metals such as gold, silver, platinum, and others have consistently been regarded as the prevailing symbol of affluence. Ancient civilizations utilized these metals for the purpose of serving as currency to facilitate their commercial exchanges. This chapter will provide you with crucial information pertaining to this particular investment instrument. Additionally, you will gain knowledge on the art of investing in precious metals as a means to augment your earnings.

Two Valuable Metallic Assets Worthy of Investment

Gold, a precious metal, is utilized in the production of exquisite jewelry items. Moreover, it has the capability to fabricate various components found in contemporary technological devices, such as computers. Gold exhibits corrosion resistance, possesses insulating properties against heat, demonstrates chemical stability, and functions as an electrical conductor.

- Platinum, a valuable metallic element, is utilized in the fabrication of components for automobiles, computer devices, and medical apparatus.

The Benefits Provided by Precious Metals

Appreciation in worth - Based on historical records, precious metals have a tendency to experience a natural appreciation in value over time. As an instance, the value of gold has exhibited a consistent upward trajectory over the course of the previous decade.

They afford the investor the opportunity to maintain personal custody of their assets – In the event that you choose to acquire precious metals in the form of bars, coins, or jewelry, you will be presented with the choice to retain possession of your investments. If one chooses to engage in the investment of stocks or bonds, it is important to note that one may solely retain possession of the contractual agreements or stockholder accords.

Safeguarding against inflation – Undoubtedly, precious metals provide a paramount advantage in terms of protecting one's wealth. Inflation exerts no influence on the aggregate value of these assets. Typically, the value of precious metals tends to remain stable (and sometimes even appreciate) during periods of heightened inflation.

Global value - The value of precious metals is ubiquitous: its market demand and price remain consistent across nearly all nations. This implies that you need not be concerned about the incessant and irrevocable oscillations within the currency exchange market.

Key Factors to Take into Account"
"Crucial Points for Your Consideration"
"Important Aspects to Bear in Mind"
"Essential Elements to Deliberate

- Assess the suitability of incorporating this type of asset in your investment portfolio - Before making a purchase of precious metals, it is essential to evaluate their compatibility with your current financial situation. Will you be employing these metals as a safeguard for your financial investments? Do you intend to utilize them as a means of stabilizing your portfolio?

- Determine the desired investment amount - After establishing your confidence in the viability of precious metals, deliberate upon the funds you are prepared to allocate. This decision is contingent upon your personal preferences and financial goals.

Nevertheless, financial experts assert that novice investors should allocate between 10% and 20% of their capital towards these precious metals.

- Consider strategic timing for asset acquisition – It is advised to exercise caution and thoroughly evaluate multiple traders before purchasing precious metals such as gold or platinum. It is important to also take into account the timing of your purchases. Would you be able to make the purchase in one single transaction for the entire quantity? Would it be more advantageous to divide it into smaller purchases? Are you capable of strategically timing your purchases in accordance with fluctuations in prices?

- In accordance with the advice of investment professionals, it is recommended to allocate your acquisitions into incremental transactions for optimal results. This is due to the fact that significant transactions entail considerable risks. Furthermore, it is advised that you refrain from endeavoring to anticipate the fluctuations in prices, as your level of knowledge and experience in this matter is insufficient.

Please ensure the selection of a reputable dealer, as it is imperative to invest your responsibly earned funds in precious metals from a credible source. This measure will assist you in preventing fraudulent individuals from taking advantage of you.

It is advisable to acquire goods from reputable dealers. These individuals possess steadfast enterprises and exemplary records of accomplishment. It is advisable to make your purchase from a dealer that operates a brick-and-mortar establishment, as numerous online vendors engage in unscrupulous practices.

Compounding Magic

Compounding is amazing. Allow me to elucidate the matter: Suppose you were to allocate a sum of $10,000 for investment purposes, with an annual interest rate of 5 percent. Over the course of several years, you refrain from utilizing any of the accrued interest and instead opt to let it accumulate and prosper. At the conclusion of the initial year, you will possess a sum of $10,500. Within the second year, your total amount will reach $11,030. By the end of the fifth year, your total amount will amount to $12,760. By the completion of the tenth year, the projected sum will amount to $16,290. Disregard the matter entirely until four decades have passed, at which point the $10,000 investment will have multiplied to an amount of $70,400. Impressive, isn't it? Now, contemplate the potential outcome if an interest rate of 25 percent were to be applied, and were to facilitate its growth over a span of 20 years. Subsequently, the sum would amount to $867,360! Given another decade, the initial amount of $10,000 would escalate to a staggering $75,231,640. That's compounding.

Indeed, one may harbor doubts regarding the feasibility of achieving a 25 percent annual return. However, it is noteworthy that, prior to the year 1999, Berkshire Hathaway managed to consistently generate annual compounded interest exceeding 30 percent for a continuous span of over three decades. These types of returns can indeed be achieved. Don't assume otherwise.

The crux of the matter lies not in the goal of making you a millionaire, but rather in illustrating the astonishing potential of compounding. By granting your investments ample time to flourish, the subsequent increase in your future value, or FV, is considerable and expedited.

Upon reconsideration of our equation, regardless of the duration of time involved, if the interest fails to reach a certain magnitude, the ultimate value will not hold substantial significance. The same principle holds true in the reverse scenario. An exorbitantly high interest rate might be in effect, but if you keep your funds invested for just a few years, your returns will be minimal.

To clarify, if one were able to devise a method that enables the attainment of progressively higher interest rates while allowing for prolonged growth of their investment, they would have the potential to achieve significant financial success. As a value-oriented investor, your responsibility entails seeking out the most favorable interest rates and subsequently maintaining the investment for an extended duration. If one cultivates a positive relationship with time, it will consequently foster a harmonious connection with money.

The Principle of 72

The principle of the rule of 72 is derived from the formula that was previously examined. It enables the determination of the duration required for the principal amount to double, taking into account the compounding interest. Once you have ascertained the rate of return, you can readily determine the timeframe required to achieve a two-fold return on your investment. Allow me to provide a concise explanation of the rule of 72:

Time required to achieve a 100% return on investment at a specified interest rate:

The value is obtained by dividing 72 by the interest rate.

The required interest rate to achieve a twofold increase in your investment over a designated time period:

The quotient of 72 divided by the number of years.

Here is the sequence in which this progresses:

With a rate of 24 percent, it would require three years to achieve a twofold increase in your investment (calculated by dividing 72 by 24).

In order to achieve a twofold increase in your investment within a span of 9 years, it is imperative to generate a minimum interest rate of 8 percent (calculated as 72 divided by 9).

With a growth rate of 10 percent, it would require a span of 7.2 years to accomplish a doubling effect (derived from dividing 72 by 10). Furthermore, to achieve a quadrupling effect, it would necessitate a time frame of 14.4 years.

Regarding the Issue of Return Rates

Consider the scenario wherein you possess a familial connection, specifically a cousin, who made a real estate investment by purchasing a property valued at $300,000. Subsequently, after a span of ten years, they managed to successfully vend the aforementioned property for a considerably higher price amounting to $1,200,000. Sounds impressive. With a growth rate of 30 percent per annum, the investment yielded a total return of 300 percent over a period of 10 years. Indeed, that statement holds true.

Nevertheless, when considering additional investments in conjunction with this one, it becomes imperative to consider the impact of compounding in order to obtain a more comprehensive understanding of the outcome. Suppose your cousin made a decision ten years ago to allocate $300,000 into an investment vehicle that facilitated the compounding of her returns. What would have been the resulting rate of return for her? Utilizing the rule of 72, one can determine that the compounded interest or rate of return would amount to a mere 14.4 percent. However, the current situation is not subpar by any means; rather, it provides a much more precise representation.

The geometric rate of return, alternatively referred to as the compounded rate of return, is synonymous with this concept. It exhibits a significant deviation from a simple calculation involving the division of the total return by the number of years taken to accumulate it, as exemplified by our 30 percent annual return. "Provided below is the methodology for computing geometric rates of return:

The compounded/geometric rate of return can be calculated by subtracting 1 from the product of [(Ending value/Beginning value) raised to the power of (1/n)].

Where 'n' denotes the value representing the number of years.

In order to compute this, analogous to the situation of your cousin, one would perform the division of $1,200,000 by $300,000, yielding a quotient of 4. Next, you would raise 4 to the power of ten multiplied by one-tenth, resulting in the value 1.149. By deducting 1 from the figure of 1.149, the resulting value equates to 14.9. This precise percentile significantly deviates from what the rule of 72 would yield. However, it is important to consider that the rule itself is merely an approximation and should not be regarded as a precise measure.

Using the rule of 72, one can expeditiously compute and determine suitable investment options, enabling a comparative analysis to identify optimal allocation for maximizing long-term rate of return on capital.

It is acceptable to be thrifty.

You have transitioned into becoming a value investor. Not a trader. Merchants are occupied engaging in the acquisition of assets at high prices, subsequently selling them for even higher prices. That's not you. The recommended approach involves acquiring assets at a lower value and subsequently selling them at a higher price, thus increasing the chances of obtaining a favorable rate of return. State that the intrinsic value of your stock amounts to $55. By purchasing it for $70, one can infer that it is predicated on the anticipation of an increase in its inherent worth or the likelihood that potential investors would be amenable to paying $85 for it. That could happen. Indeed, such occurrences are rather frequent. Nevertheless, should you have acquired the identical stock at a price of $35, you would subsequently have the opportunity to realize a growth of 50 percent when it reverts back to its inherent value of $70.

Exercise caution when considering stocks with significant return rates; thoroughly evaluate the fundamentals and growth rate to ascertain their suitability for investment. In addition to the rate of growth, you also stand to benefit from the potential returns resulting from a reversion to the underlying intrinsic values of these stocks, achieved through minimizing the cost of acquisition.

Cut Your Losses

Compounding can have adverse effects as well. Protracting your retention of negligible winners or losers can inflict significant harm upon you over an extended period. Consider a scenario where you possess an investment that yields an 8 percent return initially, but subsequently lags behind a market performer by 17 percent after a span of 10 years. This proportion increases to 31 percent after a period of 20 years, continuing to rise thereafter. That exorbitant cost is far too burdensome for investments that demonstrate lackluster performance. Regardless of the course of action you choose, diligently minimize the extent of your losses, thereby allowing yourself to concentrate on the winners.

Time Requirements

The period of time available for you to allocate towards investment is limited, and it is possible that, considering your investment choices, you may find yourself rarely monitoring your investments. If you opt for the approaches outlined in chapter two, specifically conventional investments, it is important to acknowledge that there will be an initial requirement of diligent research to identify appropriate investment avenues. However, subsequent to these preliminary endeavors, the investments are anticipated to accrue organic growth. As an illustration, should you desire engagement in dividend stocks, it is necessary to engage in diligent research regarding the dividend-paying stocks available and their frequency of payouts. Moreover, periodic monitoring of your investment, ideally on a monthly basis, is advised to safeguard against any potential depreciation.

The non-traditional investments discussed in chapter two necessitate a heightened level of exertion, primarily focusing on establishing interpersonal connections. Whether such communication pertains to establishing a real estate trust or to becoming engaged in a local enterprise, it is imperative that your investments receive heightened scrutiny, contingent upon the level of trust you place in your investment associates. Even while undertaking an investment in a local enterprise, your collaborator in this scenario would be the proprietor of the establishment, and depending on the extent of your trust, periodic evaluation of the business may be necessary. If you have limited familiarity with the proprietor, it would be advisable to establish a harmonious relationship to ensure convenient and regular monitoring of your investment.

Where to Start?

Chapter two provides optimal investment strategies tailored specifically for novice investors. Listed herein are techniques that can be employed to generate promptly attained profits while necessitating minimal initial investment. I firmly maintain that the initial point of departure holds little significance, as it is the extent of one's capital that ultimately dictates their starting position. The advanced strategies discussed in chapter three have the potential to yield immediate benefits. Operate within the parameters of the initial capital at your disposal, and you will experience favorable outcomes. Please be aware that each of the investments mentioned in this publication is considered to be relatively secure, thereby necessitating minimal levels of active supervision. One can easily invest and subsequently yield returns by adopting a passive approach.

Comprehend Your Financial Metrics

Once you have defined your financial goals, determined the desired monetary milestone, and undertaken the necessary financial literacy, the subsequent step involves familiarizing yourself with and comprehending your financial metrics in order to ascertain your current starting point.

There exist a plethora of significant personal financial metrics that one ought to acknowledge, encompassing:

⬜ Credit assessment " "⬜ Credit evaluation " "⬜ Credit scoring " "⬜ Creditworthiness assessment

• Financial worth • Economic value • Quantifiable worth

⬜ Aggregate outstanding balance

☐ Overall savings in costs

☐ Interest rates

These statistics will provide the basis for initiating your journey and will aid you in formulating a strategic approach to accomplish the specific goals you have established.

4. Create a Strategy

You have established the foundation for attaining financial prosperity, however, simply expressing a desire for wealth and analyzing statistical data will not suffice to achieve this goal.

The present moment calls for the development of a strategic plan to attain financial prosperity.

An indispensable component in the formulation of your strategy will involve the establishment or evaluation of your fiscal plan, and implementing any necessary modifications, to initiate progress toward your predetermined goals. The majority of individuals hold distaste towards budgeting, yet it is of utmost importance to possess an understanding of the financial allocation and devise a coherent plan to redirect funds towards desired destinations.

In light of everything, you must first ascertain the current location of your funds before initiating any modifications to their allocation.

Once a budget has been established, it is advisable to contemplate possible modifications, prioritize the allocation of funds, and determine the necessary actions in order to achieve the established objectives.

The allocation of your resources and the evaluation of your financial position will determine the areas to prioritize and shape the direction of your strategic approach. If you possess a deficit in your overall financial worth, it would be advisable to commence the process of debt repayment and actively pursuing savings. In the event that you possess a considerable amount of capital, it would be advisable to contemplate making investments. What strategies can be employed to enhance one's income and optimize asset growth in the presence of existing investments?

This is where the guidance of a financial coach, advisor, or even an acquaintance or colleague can prove invaluable in developing a well-structured plan of action, delineating it into realistic and attainable milestones.

5. Place Primary Focus on Minimizing Debts" "Dedicate Efforts Towards Reducing Debt" "Channel Attention towards Debt Mitigation" "Prioritize the Reduction of Debt" "Devote Considerable Effort to Alleviating Debt
The repayment of debts ought to be regarded as an essential element in the formulation of any strategy aimed at accumulating wealth.

Regrettably, the vast majority of Americans find themselves burdened by varying degrees of financial debt. Although certain forms of debt are essential (such as acquiring a home, vehicle, or educational loan), the majority of debt is a direct result of exceeding one's financial capabilities.

This is especially valid with regards to consumer indebtedness, specifically credit card indebtedness. Undoubtedly, a certain amount of credit card debt may arise from unforeseen circumstances, however, a significant portion can be attributed to excessive spending.

Irrespective of the factors contributing to one's indebtedness, it is imperative to discharge the outstanding obligations and avert further accumulation thereof, if one seeks to attain financial prosperity. Debt, along with the accompanying interest expenses, diminishes your overall financial worth, spending ability, and potential for both saving and investing.

Commence by addressing the debt with the most elevated interest rate and exert efforts to make payments exceeding the minimum requirement every month, thus expediting its complete repayment. After settling one obligation, allocate the monthly payment towards another, continuing this process until all debts with high interest rates and debts related to assets that decrease in value, like a vehicle, are fully repaid.

If you possess a mortgage, endeavor to limit it exclusively to a mortgage repayment, thus allowing you to dedicate your full attention to investing using the funds formerly allocated for payments.

Traditional vs. Turnkey: the Numbers

In the context of privately owned land, the term "market value" refers to the perceived worth of a property, which is determined by factors such as prevailing market conditions, including the level of demand, and comparing it with similar properties in the market. Using market value to evaluate the conventional and comprehensive strategies.

Conventional approach: Acquire property at a significantly lower cost than its market value, then carry out renovations on the property—these two expenses should total less than the market value of the improved property. Turnkey approach: Acquire an already completed or significantly improved property at or near its market value.

In the traditional approach, property value appreciation is achieved through the enhancement (rehabilitation) of the property. The concept of driving appreciation entails the identification and acquisition of a distressed property, followed by its strategic enhancement, resulting in a considerable increase in value that surpasses the initial investment made in its improvement. The additional value you have acquired is currently in your possession, and this has been accomplished through the process of "driving appreciation."

As an example, consider the acquisition of a distressed property for a sum of $50,000, with an additional investment of $20,000 towards its rehabilitation. It follows that the overall financial commitment towards the property amounts to $70,000. Following the period of recuperation, the current value of the property amounts to $100,000. That represents an additional $30,000 in accrued value that currently belongs to you, as you successfully generated this appreciation through the rehabilitation process.

The acquisition of a turnkey property entails payment at approximately market value, which proves advantageous as the property is already enhanced and hence excludes any possibility of making further modifications, should there be a need. Irrespective of your ability to do so, you would face considerable challenges in selling it for a substantially higher price than its market value in any case. With regard to a distressed property, given the significant disparity between its acquisition cost and market value, there exists an ample opportunity to undertake its renovation, leverage the subsequent appreciation, and eventually sell it at prevailing market value, all while retaining profitable returns.

Do you consider yourself to be the more advantageous choice? Therefore, engaging in this activity entirely is not advisable.

The numerical data exhibits a discernible improvement when employing the conventional approach compared to utilizing turnkey solutions. Hence, one may question the rationale behind purchasing a turnkey property instead of investing efforts into renovating a property independently.

Now we can delve into the core essence of this discourse.

Opt for Higher Remuneration in Exchange for Reduced Workload, or Enhance Profitability via Increased Workload?

In the majority of instances, participants in this discourse display a willingness to enhance returns through diligent effort. There is a reason why individuals assert that this is the most optimal approach to succeed in real estate investing, as it has proven effective. Nevertheless, this does not imply that hands-off strategies are ineffective.

The primary and widely recognized argument against turnkey solutions is that substantial cost savings can be achieved by personally undertaking all tasks involved. This phenomenon is manifested in two fundamental aspects concerning investment properties: economizing on the property acquisition itself by acquiring the distressed property at a substantial discount below market value, and achieving cost savings by personally assuming the role of property management instead of employing a professional property manager. Nonetheless, can it be affirmed that substantial savings are indeed being accumulated through the aforementioned self-performed activities? It depends on one's perspective.

Let us examine the costs associated with property management. Typically, a property manager levies a fee of 10% of the monthly rent as compensation for their management services rendered to the property owner. Given the assumption that your investment property generates a monthly rental income of $1,000, the cost associated with property management would amount to $100 per month. In relation to monthly earnings, each $100 holds significance due to the fact that typically one receives only several hundred dollars per month. Therefore, it is advisable for individuals to consider the idea of managing their own rental properties as a means of potentially saving $100 per month.

If you find the responsibilities of being a landlord effortless or pleasurable, without compromising your overall well-being, there is no justification for engaging a property manager, thus allowing you to retain the $100 monthly fee for yourself. Regardless, there are several considerations investors should pose when determining whether to engage in property rental.

What value do you attribute to your personal time?

To what extent do time and effort contribute to the practice of landlording?

Allow me to assume a valuation of my time at $75 per hour. This implies that, in the event that I were to undertake a task on behalf of someone, I would impose a fee amounting to $75 per hour. Given a hypothetical scenario where a property supervisor levies a monthly fee of $100 for the facilitation of landlording duties on my behalf, how does this compare with the perceived value of the time I would otherwise invest in these responsibilities?

Assuming my hourly rate is $75, it would require approximately 1.34 hours of work in order for me to earn $100. If I were to dedicate approximately 1.34 hours per month to managing my investment property, I would incur expenses equivalent to those I would pay to a property manager. Given that I dedicate less than 1.34 hours per month to fulfill my obligations as a landowner, it follows that the associated cost would be under $100. This suggests that the financial value of my role as the property manager would be exceedingly significant. However, if the responsibilities of being a landlord required a time commitment exceeding 1.34 hours per month, equivalent to a value of over $100 based on my hourly rate, it would be financially advantageous to delegate these tasks to a property director for a fee of $100, rather than personally handling them.

Is it necessary to dedicate more than 1.34 hours per month in order for a landowner to manage a property? Taking all factors into account, that is contingent upon the premises and the residents. Do you possess a property of lower value that necessitates significant repairs or a tenant demographic of inferior quality who consistently requires maintenance, damages property, or fails to fulfill rental payments? Alternatively, do you possess properties that are easily manageable and tenants who require minimal attention, leading to overall low maintenance obligations? Additionally, please be mindful that certain months may necessitate no time allocation on your part, whereas other months may necessitate a significant number of hours. What will be the standard timing? Allow me to recount an authentic narrative that transpired on one of my properties. During the period in which I had involvement in real estate investment in Nicaragua, I made frequent visits to the country. By that time, I had commenced the acquisition of rental properties, all of which were being effectively managed by professional property managers. On a particular afternoon, while leisurely positioned by the poolside of the resort, I found myself partaking in the savor of a piña colada (if I may confess, it was not my initial indulgence of the day). In this serene moment, I received a notification from my esteemed property manager in Atlanta, apprising me of a recent tempestuous occurrence. Evidently, a prevailing storm had swept through the vicinity, resulting in the partial removal of the rooftop of one of my esteemed properties. I recommended to him that he maintain his patience as I proceeded to contact my insurance agency. I contacted the insurance agency and initiated the process, providing them with the contact information of my property supervisor. This was to facilitate a site visit by their representative in order to assess the extent of the damage. I concluded the conversation with them, promptly responded to my property supervisor through a written message, notifying him that the case had been duly documented and that the designated agent would be in touch with him. He conveyed his deepest appreciation, thereby concluding the discussion. Apart from providing approval for the previous work request, I did not undertake any further actions regarding the rooftop as the property manager diligently handled all aspects of the matter with the insurance company and contractors.

A violent storm tore the roof off my residence, yet I never once found it necessary to seek shelter indoors or relinquish my grasp on the refreshing piña colada in my hand. If I had been the proprietor of the land in question, I am uncertain of the exact impact it would have had on my journey at that particular juncture. I am uncertain whether I would have promptly boarded a plane or if I could have enlisted the services of an individual from a distant location to conduct an inspection. However, I am certain that, at the very least, the task list pertaining to the roof would have resembled something along the lines of:

Engage in effective dialogue with residents in order to discuss provisional resolutions, as well as provide timely updates on the contractors' forthcoming activities.

collaborate with the insurance adjuster

Convene with the insurance adjuster onsite

Procure the services of a reputable contractor for the project.

Oversee the contractor responsible for the completion of the task.

What would be the total duration in hours for this task? I can't really understand. However, I am aware that it ultimately represents more than just the five minutes I spent in the pool to organize all of that work.

In addition to exchanging my time for monetary compensation, there is an additional notion encompassed within this context. What can be posited concerning the aforementioned third currency - mental stability? Cease your concern regarding the duration of time that would have been required for me to oversee the management of this property's highest point, and the act of departing Nicaragua in order to accomplish it. Instead, acknowledge the contrasting feelings of anxiety associated with managing and similar obligations, in comparison to the tranquility experienced by remaining in the pool without any such worries.

I am aware that the detriment to my mental well-being while fulfilling the duties of a landlord does not outweigh the benefit of having an additional $100 per month in my financial account. However, there are individuals who do not find the responsibilities of being a landlord burdensome and believe the effort is justified in order to accrue an additional $100 in monthly income without any adverse psychological impact. This will also serve as an opportunity to explore broader contribution methods—certain individuals will not mind undertaking a wide range of tasks and may even derive enjoyment from it, whereas others may strongly disapprove of such responsibilities. It is not imperative to emphasize the selection of a particular course; rather, it is essential to comprehend the array of options available and discern the one that aligns most suitably with your needs. Every investor must assess the financial logistics and quality of life logistics on an individual basis, recognizing that each investor and each situation will vary.

The matter at hand is that a considerable number of individuals fail to comprehend that there exist methods to become a financial supporter without having to undertake an excessive amount of labor. It is preferential to steer clear of all such instructional manuals.

There are also various factors to consider when determining whether or not you wish to assume sole responsibility for all tasks pertaining to your properties.

Ascertain The Desired Lifestyle

When it comes to lifestyles, having a well-defined notion of your desired way of life forms the foundation of your investment timeline. There is no inherent flaw in harboring ambitious dreams. Nevertheless, it is crucial for you to comprehend that attaining financial independence entails funding your chosen way of life without the necessity of engaging in continuous employment. For certain individuals, the concept of "indefinite" may encompass the entirety of their existence. In the context of others, it may simply entail availing themselves of an unrestricted amount of time.

To determine the required funds for supporting your lifestyle, it merely entails analyzing the numerical data. Take your current lifestyle. Utilize it as a foundation. Calculate the cumulative sum of your monthly expenditures. Make every effort to encompass all of your expenditures. The more comprehensive the level of detail, the higher the level of precision in determining the number.

Now, for the purpose of this analysis, let us consider a monthly figure of $1,000. Hence, it would be necessary for you to generate a monthly income of $1,000 to adequately fund your chosen way of living. This is your baseline.

The subsequent course of action entails determining the desired lifestyle. In order to determine this figure, it is necessary to ascertain the financial implications of sustaining this lifestyle. You will be required to calculate the cumulative expenses associated with the given situation, and subsequently determine a numerical value. Let us consider, hypothetically, that your desired way of life would incur expenses amounting to $2,000. Therefore, you would be required to initially generate a sum of $1,000 in order to attain financial independence, subsequently followed by the need to generate $2,000 to attain your desired lifestyle.

Calculating Financial Independence
To ascertain the duration required for achieving financial independence, one must consistently attain the necessary monetary figure to sustain their chosen lifestyle. Once an individual achieves a consistent level of financial solvency that allows them to sustain their desired lifestyle, they can ascertain their attainment of that goal. Therefore, if you can generate a consistent sum of $1,000 over a period of three successive months, as illustrated in our example, it can be inferred that you have achieved the desired target.

Let us consider a hypothetical scenario where your investment yields a monthly return rate of 5%. Therefore, in order to generate a profit of $1,000, a monthly investment of $20,000 would be required. A $20,000 investment yielding a 5% return would amount to $1,000. If you currently possess $20,000, it will require a few months to generate this level of return. However, assuming an initial capital of $1,000, it would require several months to attain such a level of returns.

To arrive at a reasonably precise figure, let us consider a 5% yield on an initial investment of $1,000. That's $50. Additionally, proceed by combining your earnings with the capital you have invested. Therefore, in the second month, it would be advisable to allocate a total amount of $1,050 towards your investment. With a 5% rate of return, the second month's earnings would amount to $52.50. In the third month, an investment of $1,102.50 would be made.

In this instance, we are employing minimal numerical values and assuming exceedingly cautious yields. However, it demonstrates the kind of computation you must undertake in order to achieve your intended objective. It is essential to bear in mind the primary objective, which is to refrain from withdrawing your profits within the initial few months. By consistently reinvesting your investments on a monthly basis, you will gradually accumulate your investment capital. Within a short span of time, you will amass a substantial amount of capital to utilize. This will significantly enhance the feasibility of attaining your desired objective.

2.2 What Are the Reasons for Your Crypto Investments?

An exploration of the reasons for investing at present will initiate each argument with the phrase currently.

Currently, there exists limited competition within the market. Are you taken aback? That is correct. Indeed, there is a continuous increase in the level of concern regarding this matter, albeit the extent of rivalry remains relatively limited. Up to this point, this market has remained unregulated. This can be attributed to the previously mentioned circumstance, wherein a majority of individuals exhibit caution towards novel trends and undertakings.

Furthermore, the current state of this market presents a lucrative opportunity for financial gain. Despite being in the nascent stages of development, there is still potential to earn a substantial income from cryptocurrency prices. If you possess the ability to effectively manage risks, it is plausible to accumulate wealth gradually.

Furthermore, it is worth noting that the current market is inundated with a significant proportion of individuals who partake without contributing their fair share. They enter the cryptocurrency market with the sole objective of making quick monetary gains, without making any effort to acquire knowledge about it. Commonly, these individuals tend to come from pyramid schemes operated by self-proclaimed "experts" who offer guidance without possessing substantial practical knowledge in the respective domain. I must give due recognition to the fact that the market provided support to these individuals initially, affording them the chance to amass substantial wealth. Nevertheless, should you aspire to achieve comparable outcomes within the current bitcoin market, considerable effort will need to be invested.

Lastly, one can observe a scarcity of risks prevailing in the market. The majority of individuals anticipated the day, five years ago, when bitcoin would be officially prohibited. In recent years, numerous nations across the globe have recognized the significance of bitcoin. Cryptocurrency has garnered significant momentum that renders it unstoppable at this point. Do you sincerely hold the belief that this does not serve as a clear manifestation of the ability to invest your funds without the concern of encountering numerous constraints and limitations?

Prior to proceeding, it is advisable to examine the Tesla corporation rather than solely focusing on market regulations as a means to assess the future trajectory of cryptocurrencies. According to experts, the current assessment suggests that the cost of a Tesla is prohibitively high, to the extent that it would take approximately 300 years to recover the initial investment.

For what reason, then, do informed specialists attribute such great importance to Tesla? Let us endeavor to ascertain a resolution.

Contemporary electric vehicles are characterized by their aesthetically appealing designs and modern sensibilities. However, they also exhibit a higher price point and limited practicality. However, professionals remain indifferent towards the present day. They envision a forthcoming era that could potentially materialize within the span of the ensuing two to three decades. It is challenging to envision the conventional motor vehicles that are currently prevalent on our streets in the years that lie ahead. In the upcoming years, it is possible that you may encounter your previously cherished automobile, however, I envisage a future where more sophisticated modes of transportation, like semi-flying vehicles equipped with solar panels, prevail. As a result of this, the future of electric vehicles appears promising, with Tesla poised to achieve a predominant market position.

There appears to be a lack of certainty among individuals regarding Tesla's ability to sustain its market position over the next two to three decades. However, a considerable number of individuals hold the firm belief that it will indeed succeed, consequently driving their fervent inclination to invest in the company.

Consequently, it is unequivocal that Tesla will establish a monopolistic presence within the automotive manufacturing sector over the course of the next two decades.

www.ingramcontent.com/pod-product-compliance
Lightning Source LLC
Chambersburg PA
CBHW071648210326
41597CB00017B/2150